To my friend Kathryn,
I immediately thought of
you when I saw this little
book. Even the illustrations
reminded me of your beautiful
work.
Much love,
Leslie

FEAR NOT

Compilation copyright © 2002 by Benjamin Darling.
Illustrations copyright © 2002 by Michael Woloschinow.

All rights reserved. No part of this book may be reproduced
in any form without written permission from the publisher.

Library of Congress Cataloging-in-Publication Data available.

ISBN 0-8118-3618-5

Manufactured in China.

Designed by Kristen M. Nobles.

Distributed in Canada by Raincoast Books
9050 Shaughnessy Street
Vancouver, British Columbia V6P 6E5

10 9 8 7 6 5 4 3 2 1

Chronicle Books LLC
85 Second Street
San Francisco, California 94105

www.chroniclebooks.com

Fear Not

Thoughts on Courage

Compiled by BENJAMIN DARLING

CHRONICLE BOOKS
SAN FRANCISCO

Thanks to the human heart by which we live.
Thanks to its tenderness, its joys, and fears.

—*William Wordsworth*

I've been absolutely terrified every moment
of my life and I've never let it keep me from doing
a single thing I wanted to do.

—*Georgia O'Keeffe*

A good laugh and a long sleep—the best cures of all.

—*Irish Proverb*

When in doubt, do the courageous thing.

—*Jan Smuts*

I am not afraid of storms,
for I am learning how to sail my ship.

—*Louisa May Alcott*

There is something sublime about the beginning of a new day. Possibly the previous night had been filled with dark misgivings, disappointments and oppressive fears. But the fresh beginning of a new day, with its beautiful light and its promise of unexplored possibilities, should gladden the heart and inspire the soul.

—Grenville Kleiser

Act as if it were impossible to fail.

—*Dorothea Brande*

Be bold and courageous.
When you look back on your life, you'll regret
the things you didn't do more than the ones you did.

—*H. Jackson Brown, Jr.*

Courage [is] the determination not to be overwhelmed
by any object, that power of the mind capable of
sloughing off the thingification of the past.

—*Martin Luther King, Jr.*

Never let your head hang down. Never give up
and sit and grieve. Find another way. And don't pray
when it rains if you don't pray when the sun shines.

—*Satchel Paige*

Puff, puff, chug, chug, went the Little Blue Engine.
"I think I can—I think I can—I think I can—
I think I can—I think I can—I think I can—I think
I can—I think I can." Up, up, up. Faster and faster
and faster and faster the little engine climbed, until
at last they reached the top of the mountain. Down
in the valley lay the city. . . And the Little Blue Engine
smiled and seemed to say as it puffed steadily down the
mountain, "I thought I could. I thought I could. . . ."

—Watty Piper

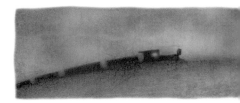

Courage is the price that life exacts for granting peace.

—*Amelia Earhart*

Courage is being scared to death—
and saddling up anyway.

—*John Wayne*

Mean old Mother Goose
Lions on the loose
They don't frighten me at all
I go boo
Make them shoo.

—*Maya Angelou*

Fear of the future is worse than one's present fortune.

—*Quintilian*

Do not think that courage lies only
in boldness and power. The highest courage
is the courage to be higher than your rage and
to love a person who has offended you.

—*Persian Wisdom*

It is not hard to live through a day
if you can live through a moment.

—*Andre Dubus*

Courage consists not in blindly overlooking danger,
but in meeting it with the eyes open.

—*Jean Paul*

When it comes to the pinch, human beings are heroic.

—*George Orwell*

Someone once asked prizefighter James J. Corbett
what was the most important thing a man must do to
become a champion. He replied, "Fight one more round."

—*Unknown*

My undissuaded heart I hear
Whisper courage in my ear.

—*Robert Louis Stevenson*

Courage: Fear that has said its prayers.

—*Unknown*

Just for today I will be unafraid. Especially I will not
be afraid to enjoy what is beautiful, and to believe
that as I give to the world, so the world will give to me.

—*Unknown*

Fear less, hope more. Eat less, chew more. Talk less, say more.
Love more, and all good things will be yours.

—*Swedish Proverb*

Today I refuse to spend time worrying about
what might happen—it usually doesn't.
I am going to spend time making things happen.

—*Gerald B. Klein*

Facing it—always facing it—
that's the way to get through. Face it!

—*Joseph Conrad*

Just as man shudders with horror when he thinks
he has trodden on a serpent, but laughs when he
stoops and sees it is only a rope, so I discovered
one day that what I was calling "I" is not apparent,
and all fear and anxiety vanished with my mistake.

—*Gautama*

We all fear what we don't know—it's natural.

—*Leo Buscaglia*

Courage is not the towering oak that sees storms come and go; it is the fragile blossom that opens in the snow.

—*Alice Mackenzie Swaim*

The future is called "perhaps," which is the only possible thing to call the future. And the important thing is not to allow that to scare you.

—*Tennessee Williams*

A difficult situation can be handled in two ways:
We can either do something to change it, or face it.
If we can do something, then why worry and get
upset over it—just change it. If there is nothing
we can do, again, why worry and get upset over it?
Things will not get better with anger and worry.

—*Shantideva*

Adversity makes a jewel of you.

—*Japanese Proverb*

No matter how irrational we may know any particular fear
to be, we need to treat our fearful feelings with respect.

—*Sheldon Kopp*

Fears, Feeling but once the fires of nobler thoughts,
Fly, like the shapes of clouds we form, to nothing.

Great self-destruction follows upon unfounded fear.

—Ursula K. Le Guin

The man whose heart and mind are not at rest is
without wisdom or the power of contemplation;
who doth not practice reflection, hath no calm;
and how can a man without calm obtain happiness?

—*Bhagavad-Gita*

With the fearful strain that is on me night and day,
if I did not laugh I should die.

—*Abraham Lincoln*

Serenity comes not alone by removing the
outward causes and occasions of fear, but by
the discovery of inward reservoirs to draw upon.

—*Rufus M. Jones*

Fear knocked at the door.
Faith answered.
No one was there.

—*On the front of the mantel in the ancient Hind's Head Hotel at Bray, England*

No longer forward nor behind
I look in hope or fear;
But, grateful, take the good I find,
The best of now and here.

—*John Greenleaf Whittier*

Fear is a great inventor.

—*French Proverb*

Worry is interest paid on trouble before it becomes due.

—*Dean Inge*

Fear is the mother of safety.

—*Sir H. Taylor*

Tomorrow there will be another wind blowing.

—*Japanese Proverb*

If there is one door in the castle you have been told
not to go through, you must. Otherwise you'll just be
rearranging furniture in rooms you've already been in.

—*Anne Lamott*

Fear cannot live with faith.

—*Charles G. Adams*

In the presence of nature a wild delight runs through
the man, in spite of real sorrows.

—*Ralph Waldo Emerson*

Life shrinks or expands according to one's courage.

—*Anaïs Nin*

Virtue is bold, and goodness never fearful.

—*William Shakespeare*

Freedom of will is the ability to do gladly
that which I must do.

—*Carl Jung*

Books also give me courage . . .
to take chances, make mistakes, to explore the
world outside and within, to grow and change.

—*Elizabeth Winthrop*

It is necessary to recoil, but it is necessary to leap,
and perhaps one only recoils in order to leap better.

—*Georges Bataille*

Do what you can—and the task will rest lightly in your hand, so lightly that you will be able to look forward to the more difficult tasks which may be awaiting you.

—*Dag Hammarskjöld*

Everyone has it within his power to say, this I am today, that I shall be tomorrow.

—*Louis L'Amour*

He who sees his life as a process of spiritual perfection
does not fear external events.

—*Leo Tolstoy*

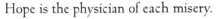

Hope is the physician of each misery.

—*Irish Proverb*

The first and great commandment is:
Don't let them scare you.

—*Elmer Davis*

There's never a trouble that comes to stay,
There's never a grievance but fades away;
Forget the heart-ache and bravely lend
A helping hand to some sadder friend.

—*Unknown*

We are terrified by the idea of being terrified.

—*Friederich Nietzsche*

Be you still, trembling heart;
Remember the wisdom out of the old days:
Him who trembles before the flame and the flood,
And the winds that blow through the starry ways,
Let the starry winds and the flame and the flood
Cover over and hide, for he has no part
With the lonely, majestical multitude.

—W. B. Yeats

To be courageous requires no exceptional qualifications, no magic formula, no special combination of time, place, and circumstance. It is an opportunity that sooner or later is presented to us all.

—John F. Kennedy

Nothing in life is to be feared. It is only to be understood.

—Marie Curie

Anxiety is the fear of fear.

—*Paul Foxman*

The first thing to do is to get control of the glance.
The next is to get control of the feelings.
And the third is to get control of the consciousness.

—*Pir Vilayat Khan*

My theory has always been, that if we are to dream,
the flatteries of hope are as cheap, and pleasanter
than the gloom of despair.

—*Thomas Jefferson*

Life's greatest achievement is the continual remaking
of yourself so that at last you know how to live.

—*Unknown*

I think laughter may be a form of courage. . . .
As humans we sometimes stand tall and look
into the sun and laugh, and I think we are never
more brave than when we do that.

—*Linda Ellerbee*

To be courageous, you must pass through the fear.

—*Todd Wilkerson*

The rudder is given into the hand of man in his frail skiff,
not that he may be at the mercy of the waves, but that
he may follow the dictates of a will directed by intelligence.

—*J. W. Von Goethe*

Feel the fear and do it anyway.

—*Unkown*

Fear nothing, for every renewed effort raises all
former failures into lessons, all sins into experiences.

—*Katherine Tingley*

The most reliable and useful courage is that which arises
from the fair estimation of the encountered peril.

—*Herman Melville*

Piglet was so excited at the idea of being useful
that he forgot to be frightened any more.

—*A. A. Milne*

Fear not for the future, weep not for the past.

—*Percy Bysshe Shelley*

Courage of soul is necessary for the triumphs of genius.

—Mme. De Staël

The fishermen know that the sea is dangerous and
the storm terrible, but they have never found these dangers
sufficient reason for remaining ashore.

—Vincent Van Gogh

What boots it to wear out the soul with anxious thoughts?

—T'ao Yuan-Ming

The world is full of happiness, and plenty to go round,
if you are only willing to take the kind that comes your way.
The whole secret is being *pliable*.

—Jean Webster

Courage isn't a brilliant dash,
A daring deed in a moment's flash;
It isn't an instantaneous thing
Born of despair with a sudden spring.
But it's something deep in the soul of man
That is working always to serve some plan.

—*Edgar A. Guest*

Let us not look back in anger,
or forward with fear, but around in awareness.

—*James Thurber*

Acceptance makes any event put on a new face.

—*Henry S. Haskins*

We must travel in the direction of our fear.

—*John Berryman*

He who fears to suffer, already suffers from fear.

—*French Proverb*

Fear not the confusion outside of thee, but that within thee; strive after unity, but seek it not in uniformity; strive after repose, but through the equipoise, not through the stagnation of thy activity.

—*Friedrich von Schiller*

Fear makes the wolf bigger than he is.

—*German Adage*

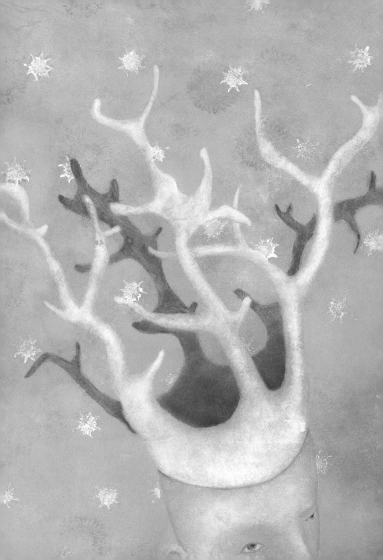

Courage is resistance to fear, mastery of fear—
not absence of fear.

—*Mark Twain*

He has not learned the lesson of life
who does not every day surmount a fear.

—*Ralph Waldo Emerson*

You must go on, I can't go on, I'll go on.

—*Samuel Beckett*

When you get into a tight place and everything
goes against you, till it seems as though you could
not hold on a minute longer, never give up then,
for that is just the place and time the tide will turn.

—*Harriet Beecher Stowe*

Every little yielding to anxiety is a step away
from the natural heart of man.

—*Japanese Proverb*

Everybody is all right really.

—*A. A. Milne*

We fail!
But screw your courage to the sticking-place and we'll not fail.

—*William Shakespeare*

To let go is to fear less—and to love more.

—*Unknown*

The best reason for holding your chin up when in trouble
is that it keeps the mouth closed.

—*Ivern Boyett*

A ship in the harbor is safe,
but that is not what ships are built for.

—*William G. T. Shedd*

Tell your heart that the fear of suffering is worse than
the suffering itself. And no heart has ever suffered
when it goes in search of its dream.

—*Paulo Coelho*

Considering how dangerous everything is,
nothing is really very frightening!

—*Gertrude Stein*

A warrior never worries about his fear. Instead, he
thinks about the wonders of *seeing* the flow of energy!
The rest is frills, unimportant frills.

—*Carlos Castaneda*

It's like the smarter you are, the more things can scare you.

—*Katherine Paterson*

When we begin to take our failures non-seriously,
it means we are ceasing to be afraid of them. It is of
immense importance to learn to laugh at ourselves.

—*Katherine Mansfield*

The most realistic attitude we can cultivate is to
hope for the best but be prepared for the worst.
If the worst does not happen, then everything is fine,
but if it does occur, it will not strike us unawares.

—*The Dalai Lama*

What a new face courage puts on everything.

—*Ralph Waldo Emerson*

The way to develop self-confidence
is to do the thing you fear, and get a record
of successful experiences behind you.

—*William Jennings Bryan*

We have to start teaching ourselves not to be afraid.

—*William Faulkner*

It is not that you must be free from fear. The moment you try to free yourself from fear, you create a resistance against fear. Resistance, in any form, does not end fear. What is needed, rather than running away or controlling or suppressing or any other resistance, is understanding fear; that means, watch it, learn about it, come directly into contact with it. We are to learn about fear, not how to escape from it, not how to resist it through courage and so on.

—J. Krishnamurti

If the doors of perception were cleansed,
everything would appear to man as it is, infinite.

—*William Blake*

Life is easier to take than you'd think. All that is
necessary is to accept the impossible, do without the
indispensable, and bear the intolerable.

—*Kathleen Norris*

The only courage that matters is the kind that gets you from one minute to the next.

—*Mignon McLaughlin*

It is best not to say, "Go away, Fear. I don't like you. You are not me." It is much more effective to say, "Hello Fear. How are you today?"

—*Thich Nhat Hanh*

In the midst of winter, I found there was within me,
an invincible summer.

—*Albert Camus*

It is perfectly true, as philosophers say, that life must be
understood backwards. But they forget the other proposition,
that it must be lived forwards.

—*Sören Kierkegaard*

On you will go
Onward up many
a frightening creek,
though your arms may get sore
and your sneakers may leak.

—*Dr. Seuss*

Fear isn't cowardice. Cowardice is failure to fight fear.
The man of courage feels fear and fights.

—*Arnold H. Glasow*

Not all who hesitate are lost.

—*Joseph Campbell*

Fall seven times, stand up eight.

—*Japanese Proverb*

Human beings are born with just two basic fears.
One is the fear of loud noises. The other is the fear of falling.
All other fears must be learned.

—*Ronald Rood*

If you ain't got a choice, be brave.

—*American Proverb*

There is no terror in a bang, only in the anticipation of it.

—*Alfred Hitchcock*

The more you try to avoid suffering the more you suffer,
because smaller and more insignificant things begin to
torture you in proportion to your fear of being hurt.

—*Thomas Merton*

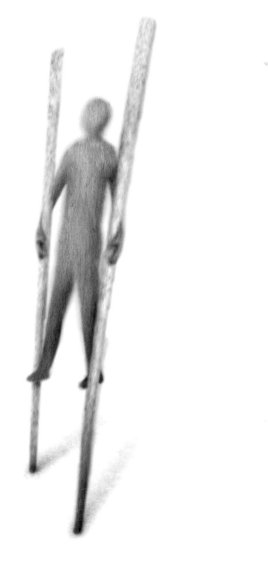

If you're afraid of the dark . . . Remember the night rainbow.

—*Cooper Edens*

Fears are educated into us,
and can, if we wish, be educated out.

—*Dr. Karl Menninger*

Never bear more than one kind of trouble at a time.
Some people bear three—all they have had,
all they have now, and all they expect to have.

—*Edward Everett Hale*

There is often less danger in the things we fear
than in the things we desire.

—*John Churton Collins*

The best way out of a difficulty is through it.

—*Unknown*

I steer my bark with hope in my heart, leaving fear astern.

—*Thomas Jefferson*

Only the dreamer can change the dream.

—*John Logan*

I am an old man and have known a great many troubles,
but most of them have never happened.

—*Mark Twain*

Fear is a question: What are you afraid of, and why? Just as the seed of health is in illness, because illness contains information, our fears are a treasure house of self-knowledge if we explore them.

—*Marilyn Ferguson*

I am not afraid of tomorrow,
for I have seen yesterday and I love today.

—*William Allen White*

For nowhere can a mind find a retreat more full of peace
or more free from care than his own soul.

—*Marcus Aurelius*

But he, whose noble soul its fear subdues,
And bravely dares the danger nature shrinks from.

—*Joanna Baillie*

Fear comes from uncertainty.
When we are absolutely certain, whether of our worth
or worthlessness, we are almost impervious to fear.

—*William Congreve*

A great part of courage is the courage
of having done the thing before.

—*Ralph Waldo Emerson*

To want less fear in the world must mean to want
more people in it who are capable of love.

—*Bonaro W. Overstreet*

Let's fear no storm, before we feel a show'r.

—*Michael Drayton*

Let me not pray to be sheltered from dangers,
But be fearless in facing them.
Let me not beg for the stilling of my pain,
But for the heart to conquer it.
Let me not crave in anxious fear to be saved,
But hope for the patience to win my freedom.

—*Dr. Rabindranath Tagore*

To fear is one thing. To let fear grab you by the tail
and swing you around is another.

—*Katherine Paterson*

Helplessness is the enemy of happiness and the ally of fear. A vital element of feeling happy is having a sense of control, of being free to shift your attention to the things that are important to you and mold your behavior accordingly.

—*Rush W. Dozier, Jr.*

Worry is a funky luxury when a lot has to be done.

—*Melvin Peebles*

Courage is a present from God or the universe to every single one of us. No matter how *uncourageous* you may feel, you're no exception—courage is inside you too.

—*Sarah Quigley* and *Marilyn Shroyer*

We must act in spite of fear . . . not because of it.

—*Unknown*

The problem of life is to change worry into thinking and anxiety into creative action.

—*Harold B. Walker*

Once men are caught up in an event they cease to be afraid. Only the unknown frightens men.

—*Antoine de Saint-Exupéry*

The best way to deal with the panic is replace it.
It is in this context that laughter—and the positive
emotions in general—perform a useful function.

—Norman Cousins

Keep your fears to yourself,
but share your courage with others.

—Robert Louis Stevenson

Most of the fear that spoils our life comes from
attacking difficulties before we get to them.

—Dr. Frank Crane

Victory over fear is the first spiritual duty of man.

—*Nicholas Berdyaev*

Your pain is the breaking of the shell
that encloses your understanding.

—*Kahlil Gibran*

Be not afraid of life. Believe that life is worth living
and your belief will help create the fact.

—*William James*

If you let fear of consequence prevent you from
following your deepest instinct, then your life will
be safe, expedient and thin.

—*Katharine Butler Hathaway*

The principle which is most potent of all to dispel fear; it is the saturation of the mind by the sense of obligation to right until it becomes second nature, so that the motives for cowardice do not enter the mind.

—Tom A. Williams

It is good to remember that the tea kettle, although up to its neck in hot water, continues to sing.

—Unknown

You gain strength, courage and confidence by every experience in which you really stop to look fear in the face. You are able to say to yourself, "I have lived through this horror. I can take the next thing that comes along." You must do the thing you think you cannot do.

—*Eleanor Roosevelt*

Although the world is full of suffering, it is also full of the overcoming of it.

—*Helen Keller*

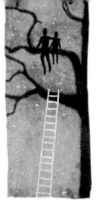

Instead of worrying unnecessarily about the future,
do what can be done now in making fuller use of
your potential. Remember, the present is the child
of the past, and the parent of the future.

—K. Sri Dhammananda

Fear is one part of prudence.

—Thomas Fuller

Since we are capable of change and modifications,
the future will be in many ways only as good as
we have the courage to make it.

—June Tapp

Fear rightly used is the father of courage
and the mother of safety.

—Henry H. Tweedy

Courage is a special kind of knowledge: the knowledge
of how to fear what ought to be feared and how
not to fear what ought not to be feared.

—David Ben-Gurion

"I Can't" hangs by a feeble grip,
"I Can" holds on with forceful hand;
"I Can't" lets all his chances slip,
"I Can" bends all to his command.

—*Annie L. Muzzey*

The art of life lies in a constant
readjustment to our surroundings.

—*Okakura Kakuzo*

"Whiniver I read in a sermon," said Mr. Dooley, "that the wurruld is going to pot, that th' foundations of government is threatened, that the whole fabric iv civilized s'ciety is in danger, that humanity is on th' down grade, and morality is blinkin', that men ar-re becomin' drunkards, an' women gamblers, an' that th' future iv th' race is desthruction, I can always console mesilf with wan thought."

"What's that?" asked Mr. Hennessey.

"It isn't so," said Mr. Dooley.

—*Finley Peter Dunne*

Out of the earth, the rose,
Out of the night, the dawn:
Out of my heart, with all its woes,
High courage to press on.

—*Laura Lee Randall*

When thinking won't cure fear, action will.

—*W. Clement Stone*

I have not ceased being fearful, but I have ceased to let fear control me. I have accepted fear as a part of life, specifically the fear of change, the fear of the unknown, and I have gone ahead despite the pounding in the heart that says: turn back, turn back, you'll die if you venture too far.

—Erica Jong

If you want to conquer fear, don't sit at home and think about it. Go out and get busy.

—Dale Carnegie

Fear gives sudden instincts of skill.

—Samuel Taylor Coleridge

When fear seizes, change what you are doing.
You are doing something wrong.

—Jean Craighead George

Humor acts to relieve fear.

—Dr. William F. Fry, Jr.

It is the lot of man to suffer, is also his fortune to forget.

—Benjamin Disraeli

Fear not to-morrow's mischance.

—Turkish Proverb

Once more read thine own breast aright
And thou hast done with fears.

—*Matthew Arnold*

Make the best use of what is in your power,
and take the rest as it happens.

—*Epictetus*

What doesn't kill me, makes me stronger.

—*Albert Camus*

Life is either a daring adventure or nothing.

—*Helen Keller*

Bravery is fear sneering at itself.

—*Maxwell Bodenheim*

The first duty for a man is still that of subduing Fear.

—*Thomas Carlyle*

Whenever conscience commands anything,
there is only one thing to fear, and that is fear.

—*St. Theresa of Avila*

Our fears are always more numerous than our dangers.

—*Seneca*

Thou hast only to follow the wall far enough
and there will be a door in it.

—*Marguerite de Angeli*

Your worst enemy cannot harm you as much
as your own mind, unguarded. But once mastered,
no one can help you as much.

—*Buddha*

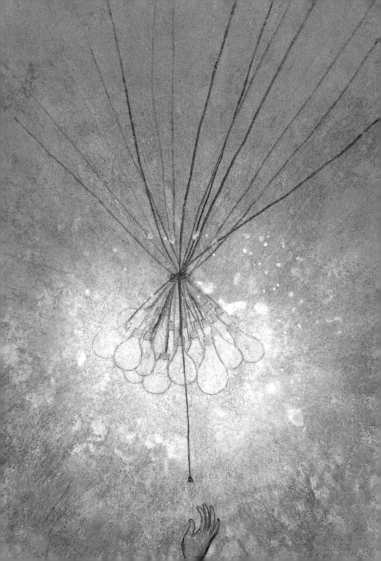

What makes the flag on the mast to wave!
. . . Courage!
What makes the elephant charge his tusk
In the misty mist or the dusky dusk?
What makes the muskrat guard his musk?
. . . Courage!

—*The Cowardly Lion from* The Wizard of Oz